The Right Choice

Choosing a College and Why it Matters

by
John J. Jackson, PhD

Copyright

ISBN13: 978-0-9884306-8-6

Jessup University Press, 2019

A catalog record for this book is

available through the Library of

Congress. Printed in the United

States of America

Dedication

It has been a great joy to write this little book on behalf of all the parents and students who are making the life changing decision on where to go to college. In recent years, the cost and value of a college education has been called into question by many in our culture. Because of my deep and abiding commitment to the families, it has been a tremendous joy to watch and support the family units (sometimes involving as many as 15-20 people!) agonize and process the choices that college presents. This little book was written in a conversational style in hopes that you will be encouraged and supported on your journey.

I prayed over this manuscript and each word that was written. If you are a student, I want you to know that I thought of your kitchen, your living room, your car, the coffee or tea shop, or the mall where you will be talking with your family and friends about this choice. Don't give up! You will make a great choice and you can do this!

Thank you for allowing me to be part of this journey. I'd like to dedicate this book to my amazing wife Pam, my children and their spouses (Derek & Jennifer, Cheyne & Dena, Zach & Rachel, Joshua, Harrison) and my grandchildren (Brooklyn, Rylee, and Skylar). I love that we have grandkids and think we may be helping them navigate this decision themselves some day as well!

You are not alone. There are a host of people who care deeply about you. One of them may have bought you this little book. My hope is that this will be the little book that has a big impact on your life. Let's start the conversation!

Acknowledgements

I want to thank the Board of Trustees, Executive Team, Faculty & Staff, and the Students of William Jessup University (www.jessup.edu). These past many years, it has been my joy to help shape and enjoy the development of Jessup as a Premier Christ-Centered University. The entire Jessup family has been a team of hope filled people who have been willing to invest heavily to see Jessup become all that God wants us to be. I want to particularly thank Pat Gelsinger, Mike West, and Cliff Daugherty who have served as Board Chairs during these exciting past several years.

I want to also thank the many private college colleagues who have graciously shared their journey in this role. When I became a college president, all I knew for certain was that I was unqualified; thankfully I have benefitted from the consistent and selfless input from colleagues who are far ahead of me in the journey.

I am grateful to my dad (in heaven with Jesus) and mom, my brothers and my sister and their amazing spouses and families, and my wife's family. It is the strength of our extended family that gives me such great encouragement in life.

Finally, I want to thank the men and women in the various churches and ministries that I have been privileged to lead and serve with over the past four (!) decades. Many pastors and community leaders have invested in and partnered with me over the years as well. I'm always built up by the gifts and heartbeat of the people I've been fortunate to have as friends, mentors, and partners; you know who you are. Thank you.

What Other People are Saying...

Honest. Practical. Immediately useful. *The Right Choice* is my choice for inspiring my college-bound triplet teenage grandchildren to think deeper and wider about their college options. The "Decision Matrix" (Dreams, Desires, Details) is brilliant!
John Pearson, Board Governance & Management Consultant, John Pearson Associates, Inc.

Given his 40 years of pastoral experience, and almost a decade of serving as a Christian College president, John Jackson is the kind of man that any soon-to-be-college-attendee would greatly benefit from knowing. In his new book, *The Right Choice*, John distills his wealth of experience into practical knowledge and fatherly wisdom that will bring great peace to anyone who is in the process of making the big decision of where to gain their college education. In these pages, which read like a conversation with a trusted mentor, John will guide you through actionable steps to make this choice, and any future life decisions, with confidence, clarity and courage!
Kris Vallotton, Leader, Bethel Church, Redding, CA, Co-Founder of Bethel School of Supernatural Ministry. Author of twelve books, including The Supernatural Ways of Royalty, Heavy Rain and Poverty, Riches and Wealth

John Jackson understands leadership and he understands higher education, he understands the church and he understands the pulse of the rising generation. If you are a parent of a high school student who is grappling with what kind of college to attend, or you ARE that student, you will have a lot to gain by adding THE RIGHT CHOICE to your must reads.
Barry H. Corey, President of Biola University and author of Love Kindness: Discover the Power of a Forgotten Christian Virtue

John Jackson is a gift—in his words, insights, teachings, and strategies. This book will help you set yourself or your child for next level success in life.
Margaret Feinberg, author of Taste and See

The importance of the right college education cannot be understated. As many of us have experienced, choosing a college can be a life-changing choice and John's insightful book will certainly help you make wise and informed choices when it comes to the best possible college education. His decision matrix is memorable and easy to follow and his advice is practical and essential for those navigating the overwhelming details of a good college experience and outcome.

Ed Stetzer, Wheaton College

"This book is full of wisdom and practical advice for anyone facing tough decisions. I am grateful for Dr. Jackson sharing these valuable lessons in a conversational way. This book is like speaking with a trusted friend."

Brady Boyd, New Life Church, Colorado Springs Author of "Remarkable"

"I'm astonished at the lack of wisdom available to help students make one of the 5 most important decisions of their lives. John Jackson has done future generations a huge favor with this very helpful book written by one whose whole life is devoted to guiding and building into college students."

Gene Appel, Senior Pastor. Eastside Christian Church, Anaheim, CA

I live with a philosophy that I need to surround myself with wise counsel. I regularly seek out wisdom and insight from those who know more than me and have more experience than me. There are many times where I feel overwhelmed and do not know what to do. I want to make the right choice, but I am not sure what that is. In those times, I seek out those valued voices of counsel. I am a father of three children and deciding on which college to attend is a major life decision we have made and will make again. Whether you are a student or a parent, that life decision can be overwhelming and confusing. I am so grateful that Dr. John Jackson has written The Right Choice to help others navigate that season with wisdom and insight. Dr. Jackson has taken the time to write this book in order to come alongside you, like a friend and mentor, with wisdom and insight, to help you make a choice that will impact the lives of those you love the most.

Banning Liebscher, Jesus Culture Founder and Pastor

What about college? President John Jackson gives any student a framework for deciding if college is a good choice and if so what college might be the right one. He does so clearly, cutting through what is not necessary to what matters. As a leading Christian educational leader and entrepreneur, Jackson sees both the changes happening in college education and the important values that have endured and will endure. This book is an excellent guide to a big decision that must be made in confusing times!

John Mark N Reynolds PhD, President, The Saint Constantine School
Senior Fellow in the Humanities, The King's College

John Jackson has written a helpful tool for working through the myriad of complex issues that surround choosing a path and place of higher education. If you're looking for help in selecting the college that's right for you (or know someone who is), this book will provide invaluable help.

Larry Osborne, Pastor & Author, North Coast Church

As it pertains to our God ordained destiny; the right decisions will facilitate, advance, and accelerate while the wrong choices can easily obstruct, hinder and impede. The Right Choice equips the student committed to doing God's will with the necessary tools not only as it pertains to selecting the "right" school but also in living the "right" life; must read, must do!

Samuel Rodriguez, New Season Lead Pastor, NHCLC President, Author of "You Are Next!", Executive Producer "Breakthrough" The Movie

"For any complicated journey a map is indispensable...a guide for the way forward that doesn't tell you there is only one way to arrive at your destination. For parents and kids considering college, this is that book. I wish John had written this fifteen years ago. Drawing us to the intersection of dreams, desires and details, John then moves to consideration of public, private and faith-based college options. Helpful beyond words."

Nancy Ortberg, CEO of Transforming the Bay with Christ

I'll never forget my son Ben doing something that had never been done to me as the pastor of a church - he interrupted my staff meeting & handed me his acceptance letter to NYU in Manhattan! We both embraced as he wept for joy and I wept for how! It was the right decision, the right school & it has paid huge dividends. This book addresses issues that must be faced when deciding on a college. Dr Jackson has written an excellent book that every parent and prospective college student should read.

Bob Roberts, Founder NorthWood Church / Glocal.net

TABLE OF CONTENTS

The Right Choice
Choosing a College and Why it Matters

Note to the reader: Throughout this book, I have used the word "college" as shorthand for college or university. You may choose a school that is a college within a university, but for the most part, I am speaking about the institution you attend as a college without referencing the complexities and naming conventions of the ultimate place you attend to receive higher education.

Introduction

"I am so stressed! Every advertisement for a college says it is the best, my friends are going to different places, and I feel like dad and mom are just as confused as I am. The costs all seem so expensive and I'm scared to make the wrong choice and end up with a lot of debt and no future or freedom. How am I supposed to know which college to choose?"

Questions like these are part of the many disruptive experiences on life's journey. In my role as a college president, pastor, and parent, I've had this and similar conversations many times. Each time, someone is searching for the right and best answer to a question that seems freighted with destiny and uncertainty all at once.

I'd like to help you make a good decision about where to go to college. And, I think I can help you with a process that you can then use for other important life decisions as well. Along the way, my hope is to share my experience and that of hundreds of others who have made their choices and are happy with the results of their decision. This book will not take the stress out of the decision-making process, but it will give you some highway markers and guardrails to protect you on the journey. In the end, you'll make a good decision for you that your family and friends will understand and hopefully support.

Let's start by acknowledging a few things about choosing a college: First, it is one of life's most important decisions. I think that faith and marriage are more important, but college has got to be right up there with them. Second, let's be honest when we say that there is likely no one "right" decision, but what we actually are doing is choosing the option that seems the best for you and your family. Finally, because college is so expensive and the financial impact on future earnings is large, the decision seems more critical than any other you have made at this point in your life.

I also want you to know that you are not alone. You, family members involved in the conversation, friends who are at the same place in life, and a host of people who have gone on before you are all participants in the drama of choosing a college. You can learn from, lean on, and be challenged by their experiences and knowledge to help you make your ultimate choice. This book will give you lots of tips and tools as part of that conversation.

I see you down the road. Years from now, after you have had a wonderful college experience where you made 3-5 great friends that stick with you for the rest of your life and had one or two professors who imprint your worldview and skillset. I see you down the road when you may have married someone you met in college, got your first job based on an internship, or changed your entire career trajectory based on your experience in college. I see you down the road. You are full of peace and joy because you are living out who you were made to be. Choosing a college well can be a life changing choice, and this book will help you make that decision (and many others!) so that you are a person of peace down the road.

Chapter 1

The Conversation Continues

A young woman, seeking my advice and with her parents leaning in, began our conversation by saying, "I've been accepted to attend Stanford University. But I'm not sure if I should go there or come to your school. What should I do?"

As you might imagine, that was a weighty question. The answer might affect her future in ways nobody can fully understand. That conversation is a model of what I'd like to share with you. I'd like to engage you in a narrative discussion that you might have with your parents as you look at the brochures (they all look the same after a while!), the websites (they all look the same too!), and use the various college calculators that exist (and of course, those get confusing after a while as well). Along the way, I want you to understand some of my bias, so I thought I should tell you about me.

At the time of writing, I am serving as the President of a faith-based private college. I have 5 kids, 4 of whom went to faith-based private schools and one who went to a major public university. I have been a pastor for almost 40 years, so literally thousands of students have come through churches I've led and made college decisions with their family members. I've seen the sheets of paper explaining the "net cost" for the student and their families and I've had the agonizing conversations about careers and community and context of people and places. No doubt about it, the college decision journey is a challenge.

My fundamental bias about the college decision process is that it is weighty, important, should be made in partnership with people who care about you (the student) with input from experts and friends, and never based on a single factor. I like to think about the college choice conversation as a Venn diagram with intersecting circles based on Dreams, Desires, and Details.

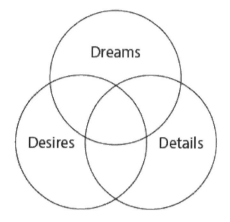

Dreams are all about your personal hopes for the future. Career, calling, sense of mission. This is where you start thinking about your life at age 30 (yikes!) and maybe even at 50 (double yikes!). If you have not done any career assessments or inventories, you can obtain one at Monster.com to benefit from that information.[1]

Desires are what you have dreamed about when you thought about college. Perhaps you have always wanted the urban alternative to your rural upbringing, the remote college setting to contrast with your suburban or city life. Did you attend a huge public high school and long for the intimacy of a tight college community? Did you long for more

---

[1] https://www.monster.com/career-advice/article/best-free-career-assessment-tools

variety, diversity, breadth of experience and travel opportunities? Each of these desires will likely shape your choice of your college.

Details include realities like tuition costs, financial aid and scholarship offers, housing costs and options, chosen major availability, and club/intramural opportunities. These details can seem mind numbing to wade through, but they affect your total cost and your experience more than you might imagine.

The convergence of your college dreams, desires, and details will provide a helpful decision matrix. Further, the remainder of this book will equip you to make this decision and others by hearing from God, clarifying your own thinking, and receiving input from trusted family and friends. This is a decision that can change your life and the process can be exciting! Let's start the journey and explore all we can together.

Chapter 2

But First, Why College?

Before we go any further, let's chat a bit about "why college."
Yes, you likely have heard that college graduates earn, on average, about a million dollars more than high school graduates over the course of their working lives. But statistics like that, which seem so ironclad, are challenged on a regular basis as society debates the cost of a college education and the debt that so often seems to accompany the journey. So, it may be that you are wondering if you really need to go the college route anyway.

Let me be the first to suggest that there are other pathways. I think that vocational / technical education pathways provide a host of options to create good potential career and financial outcomes. Many emerging Millennials and Gen Z students are trying out a variety of educational alternatives to cobble together a learning and life preparation track. Anya Kamenetz wrote *DIY U: Edupunks, Edupreneurs, and the Coming Transformation of Higher Education* in 2010 and launched a movement of sorts as the Great Recession was still unfolding. I affirm these pathways and others as potential options that you and your family should consider as part of considering your future. But the greatest way I'm equipped to serve you with in this book is to talk about why you might want to go to college, and if you do choose to do so, how you can make your best possible decision.

From my perspective as a parent, pastor, and president, I think that college is about life skills preparation and not about knowledge acquisition or vocational onboarding. I think college, at its best, equips you with the skills to know how to think, how to value, and how to communicate successfully across the broad arc of your life. Many studies tell us that people entering college will have up to 6 careers (not jobs, careers!) over the course of their life and that only 15% of the jobs that will exist by 2030 now exist according to the Institute of the Future.[2] If that is the case, how are you supposed to be prepared for an uncertain tomorrow with no clue what types of jobs will exist 20 years from when you read this?

2

https://www.huffingtonpost.ca/2017/07/14/85-of-jobs-that-will-exist-in-2030-haven-t-been-invented-yet-d_a_23030098

Based on my experience and study, there are 3 things that I like to encourage people to focus on during the college years: 1) Deepen Your Spiritual Life, 2) Cultivate Your Learning Skills, and 2) Equip Yourself for Vocation. I'll briefly unpack each of these in the next few paragraphs, but a deeper study on these subjects can be found in teaching and resources that I regularly post at my website, www.drjohnjackson.com In addition, a fellow college President named Kent Ingle has written a helpful book called A Modern Guide to College that has some good post-college tools and resources.

The young adult years are unequivocally a key time to shape and develop your spiritual life. As students take the step of leaving the umbrella of protection that parents or family have afforded them, young adulthood often means the most extensive questioning of beliefs, values, and cultural norms that has occurred up to this date. Whereas ages 15-17 might be characterized as typically involving some form(s) of rebellion against authority and "rules" structure, ages 18-24 is often characterized by a more deeply and introspectively developed holding of belief systems. At the college I lead (Jessup University), we have trained Student Life professionals who work with our faculty and develop programs to help students thrive spiritually and cultivate their personal convictions. I believe that your faith should be built up, not torn down during your college experience. Developing a faith that is deeply rooted in Scripture and a Biblical worldview equips you to discern truth and make wise value-based choices in life and is a great part of the college and young adult journey. In later chapters, we will discuss how cultivating your faith journey might look in different college contexts.

We live in a highly technical age and yet I believe more strongly than ever in the liberal arts. The liberal arts, which typically describe a curriculum rich in the Humanities, Sciences, and the Arts with the capacity for reflection, critical thinking, and effective communication, have been waning in recent years relative to both enrollments and public interest. But I think of the liberal arts in terms of outcomes: Studying the liberal arts equips you to think, read, write, and speak well. I personally believe those skills and tools will never go out of style! Further, those very skills will equip you to navigate the course of an ever-changing vocational landscape. More importantly, they are the foundational tools that, coupled with a strong Biblical worldview, will help you chart your course over the varied terrains of life.

So, I do NOT see any conflict between having a quality liberal arts education and being exceptionally employable; in fact, quite the opposite. I believe that many employers actually prioritize the very skills (critical thinking, problem solving, teamwork, creativity) that are cultivated in a study of the liberal arts. Still, in order to ensure that someone graduates from college with the capacity to take their education and couple it with "real world" experience, the college of choice has to be willing to focus its curriculum experience on real world life application.

If I could script it for you in advance, here is what I would call the "triple braided cord" for you to be exceptionally employable:

1) Engage your academic pursuits fully; progressively grasp general studies and major focus across the span of your 4 years.

2) Engage in a series of increasingly challenging and focused "real world" internships, work experience, and practical settings over your 4 years.

3) Engage with a Christ-following community of relationships where you are mentored, encouraged, held accountable, and growing, in and over time.

If you do those 3 things, you will not only be exceptionally employable at graduation, but you will have multiple options to pursue. Employers are looking for people who can think and communicate well, collaborate with others, and integrate head, heart, and hands. Pursue that plan, and you will end up there.

Let's continue our journey and look at your dreams, your desires, and the details of *The Right Choice.*

Chapter 3

Dreams Are What Stir the Heart

"I always wanted to be somebody. I just should have been more
specific." (Lily Tomlin)

"For the eyes of the LORD range throughout the earth to strengthen
those whose hearts are fully committed to Him." (II Chronicles 16:9a)

Apple Computer founder Steve Jobs once asked John Sculley of
Coca-Cola, "Do you want to spend the rest of your life selling sugared
water, or do you want to change the world?" He was talking about
computers changing the world, and indeed, they have. The genius of
Jobs, Bill Gates, and others in the computer revolution is that they saw
the needs of people, and created systems, programs, and products to meet
those needs. They didn't expect people to conform to their set-in-stone
product line. Instead, they constantly adapted their products to meet the
needs of the users. Is there a dream in your heart?

You were made to dream! In fact, God describes you as a "poem" or "masterpiece" in Ephesians 2:10. I believe that you were made to dream some "God-Size" dreams in your life. Your life has meaning and value, purpose, and impact. One of the most important things your college journey can do in your life is to help you surface, shape, and sustain a vision of how you are called to change the world. In fact, people who discover their calling in life end up being able to harness their energies and focus their life trajectory. Genuine calling is a powerful antidote to the drive to prove ourselves, the emptiness of boredom or discouragement, and the meaninglessness of superficial, scattered activities.

Is there a dream that you have been harboring in your life? Is there a thought that you've either nurtured since early childhood or perhaps kept hidden away from family and friends for fear that it would be crushed or laughed at? If so, the college decision is an important journey for you and can become the greenhouse to help your dream grow to maturity. It may be that you have not been able to spend much time dreaming or thinking about life down the road. If so, this can be an exciting season for you. I'd like to recommend 2 aspects of the dreaming journey:

1) Who am I? This is the fundamental question of "being." Answering this question of identity in terms of spiritual life, relationship with God and with others, is the central task of identity formation. Having a healthy answer to this question is absolutely key to answering the next question in a life-giving fashion.

2) Why am I here? This is the "purpose" question. This is the question of "why." Once you know who you are (and "whose" you are), then you can begin to ask very challenging questions about the purpose of your being. I usually begin to think about this in terms of a series of questions about what challenges my heart, what makes me laugh or cry and touches me at the core of my being. Ideally, your vocational pursuits should be lined up with your passion center.

If you have not been able to take a career assessment, there are many good resources available like Career Direct[3] and Christian Career Center.[4]

The truth is, you likely will have several dreams or callings over the course of your life. What is important is to cultivate the habit of listening carefully to God and to your own heart so that you can understand what your passions are. I was helped a number of years ago when I read the book *The Dream Giver* by Bruce Wilkinson. In that book, Wilkinson suggested that there was a repeated pattern in the lives of Biblical characters who pursued their dreams:

-Become aware of personal dream or calling and decide to pursue it.
-Face fear as they leave a place of comfort.
-Encounter opposition from those around them.

---

[3] https://careerdirect-ge.org/

[4]

https://www.christiancareercenter.com/professional-career-testing-for-christian-high-school-college-students/

-Endure a season of difficulty that tests their faith.

-Learn the importance of surrender and consecration to God.

-Fight the giants that stand between them and the fulfillment of their dream.

-Reach their full potential as they achieve their dream and bring honor to God.[5]

So, what is your dream? Have you been able to write out your dream on a single sheet of paper? Have you written it or printed it out so that you can put it somewhere you could reference it, refine it, and share it with others?

When you choose a college, having clarity about your dreams is a key asset. If you know your dreams, you immediately can have a bit of a filter for your college choice. Your dreams and your college's strengths should line up. Your college should have the area of study, the resources and personnel, and corporate or human connections to help you pursue

---

[5] Wilkinson, Bruce, *The Dream Giver,* Colorado Springs, Multnomah, 1984. (*(See pp. 70 ff.)*

your passion. If you do not know your dreams with clarity, you should ask if your potential college has the ability to help you discover them. If a school does not believe in helping people achieve their dreams, RUN from it! Of course, most schools will tell you that they help people fulfill their dreams. One of the reasons I encourage you to make your college visit with members of your family present is that they can help you see and understand variables and factors you might not be able to see and discern on your own if you were making a solo visit.

Chapter 4

Desires Are What I Long For

Dreams are the true "arc" of your life that flow from the passions inside your gut. Those dreams help guide the trajectory of your life as you pursue your passions and shape them into the relational and vocational future that lies ahead of you. Dreams are great, but they can often feel like they are distant and fuzzy; pictures of an uncertain though compelling future. Contrast what your dreams might feel like with desires. Desires are tangible and experiential. Desires revolve around what your hopes are that need to be translated into current reality. Desires are close enough that you can "taste" them, whereas dreams are typically far enough away so that you can only "feel" them.

Do you live in the city and have you always dreamed of exploring the countryside? Do you attend a small high school and really long to see what life is like in a bigger setting? Have you always wanted to play a particular sport, experience a specific adventure, or be part of a local or globally impacting project? Maybe you have some best friends that you want to stick with after high school as you pursue further education? All of these criteria fit under the category of "desires." Desires can be geographic, experiential, relational, or purposeful. As you ponder where you will go to college, think deeply and clearly about how each of these dimensions and how the colleges in your list stack up to them. In the paragraphs that follow, I will give brief commentary that might assist you in evaluating your options regarding desires.

For many, the implicit message is that if you want to "grow up" and "fully mature," you have to go "away" to college. This contention, often supported by public media and private conversations, serves to suggest to many that the only "real" college choice of a mature person will be to move across the country.

So, you may have noticed how many times I have used "quotes" above. The reason I did that is that I think "common knowledge" is quite frankly wrong. There may indeed be a rationale for you to move across the country to pursue your collegiate education. But did you know that 80% of college students attend college fewer than 200 miles away from their home? Further, I think there are demonstrated benefits to attend college relatively close to your family, friends, and community. Some of those benefits include the capacity to stay connected to the most likely spiritual foundations, relationships, and vocational settings for your future.

I do not believe that college has to be a 4-year bubble, but I think there is a danger of it happening if you are not careful. So, I strongly endorse the notion that you NOT eliminate a college that is close or within a few hours of your family, your church, your friends, and your likely future home. Again, there may be very appropriate and explicit reasons for you to select a college that is hundreds or thousands of miles away from your family (for instance, a specialized program of preparation), but I simply want to contend for you to not eliminate schools that are close to home.

Regarding the experiential and relational dimensions, I want to affirm your dreams of what you will get to encounter in college. If recreation, sports, clubs, travel, or any other dimension of college life is high on your list, be real and authentic about those desires. Share those desires with people you know and love and have them walk with you through the selection process and making sure you are honest about those desires. Many of your desires and hopes and dreams for college reflect you and your heartbeat and should be incorporated into your college search map. At the same time, I think it would be helpful for you to know whether your desires were created by the media experiences you have had or whether they are organically emerging in you. In my experience, some of the best things you can get from college will be 3-4 friends that you can connect with for the rest of your life and 1-2 key professors who will imprint on how you think and see the world. If you decide to attend a college because 3-4 of your great friends are going to attend the school, I do not think that is automatically a bad reason. It should not be your only reason, but it is a perfectly good reason to be considered along with all your other dreams, desires, and details.

One of the most important of your desires is what I have described as "purpose." Being purposeful is about a sense of calling. I long for that in my life and I long for you to have that as well. The Latin word for vocation is "vocare;" it means roughly to "call, to name, to invoke." I like to think of purposefulness through the lens of Ephesians 2:10 which tells us that *"For we are God's handiwork, created in Christ Jesus to do good works, which God prepared in advance for us to do."*

The Bible teaches that every one of us are made in the image of God and that our lives have meaning and value. It is clear from Scripture that meaning and value comes primarily from our identity as sons and daughters of God. But secondarily, it comes from the distinct and beautiful parts of who God made us to be. Part of why you are likely stressed and feeling the pressure of the college search is that this time of life, at least in our modern society, is in large measure defined by the search for answering the questions "Who am I?" and "Why am I here?" At its best, college is a season where you can search for the answer to that question in a safe and supportive environment and then pursue the vocation/calling that is the overflow of your identity.

In the chapters ahead, we will discuss at least a couple variations on types of college settings and how that might assist you in the search process for the right place to be purposeful.

For now, let me suggest that the college search is helped and made more complete if it is coupled with good questioning and a process about your answers to the questions I posed above (Who am I? and Why am I here?). As you might suspect, I think those questions are best asked in community, and not in isolation. Family who love you, friends who believe in you, teachers and respected leaders who are insightful about you…these are the tremendous fellow travelers that can give you input and reflection in ways that will strengthen your own sense of discovery. While it is true that a good majority of students who enter college do not "have it all figured out," if you are at least asking those questions and beginning to sense some of those answers, your college search will be made more effective.

Each college will approach the subject of purposefulness from a different paradigm (or worldview). Part of our later conversation will be to discuss how to compare and contrast your own worldview with that of the school that you choose. Understanding the prevailing worldview of the colleges you are looking at is an important dimension of your decision process and I will be equipping you for that part of your search in the chapters to come. Identifying your sense of life purpose and where you are on the journey, understanding the worldview of purposefulness that colleges you are searching have, and digesting the alignment or divergence between those 2 is an important part of successfully completing the purposefulness aspect of your college desires.

Chapter 5

Details Matter

Sigh. Ugh. Really, do we have to talk about this? If you were my teenager (my wife and I have parented 5 children through the teenage years), this is likely where the temptation for the eye roll and the distant and blank stare would begin. But, my dear friend, this subject of details is extremely important and it will affect how you live and breathe during and after the college years. So, make sure you pay attention here! What *details matter*?

The details of your college search are seemingly endless, part of why you are stressed, and part of why I am writing this book. When I think of details, I fundamentally think of tuition costs and financial aid, residential and nonresidential options, transportation, transfer credits, and major considerations. In this chapter, we will unpack each of those items briefly so that they can be added to your college search toolkit.

Tuition costs are simply the easiest thing in the whole college search process to quantify when making comparisons between schools and school types. Public college A charges B, private college C charges D, and faith-based college E charges F. A simple chart should do, right?

Well before I shatter your understanding of the simplicity of that, let me suggest that understanding tuition alone is important...but wholly insufficient. Every public college has some financial aid available, and every private and faith-based college gives generous financial aid. Until you receive an offer from each college that shows you your "net cost" to attend (typically showing you your tuition and fees less all forms of aid), you will not know your true out of pocket family cost to attend that particular school. These days, you can make general comparisons through use of popular sites such as College Navigator,[6] but even with those helpful sites, each school will have to make a specific offer to you before you know your true personal costs of attendance.

Costs of attendance are a very helpful detail and include the residential options. Many private schools require freshman and sophomore students (or alternatively, all students under the age of 21) to live on campus unless they meet specific criteria (e.g., family living in town). Private schools typically include this as part of an attempt to build community life as an essential part of the college experience. Your college selection process should include reference to the availability and

---

[6] https://nces.ed.gov/collegenavigator

desirability of nonresidential living options if you should choose that at some point in your college career. Some private and faith-based colleges are located in more remote settings where nonresidential living options are limited and this may be a factor in your choice.

Even when costs and living options are known, there is another detail that is essential to understand. That factor, known as graduation rate, is readily available on public sites (like the College Navigator site referenced previously). Graduation rate essentially means a measurement of how many "first time freshman" graduate in 4 to 6 years. The percentages that are shown will always be less than 100%. As a basic guideline, if a school does not graduate somewhere near 50% of students in 4 years and 60% of students in 6 years, it is worth asking some questions about this. Some public colleges are impacted in class sizes and some private and public colleges are serving populations of students who are either first generation or come from challenging backgrounds. Any number of factors can affect this rate, but it is an important part of the scorecard to look at and understand for your college choice list.

Transportation realities are also important for you to understand as part of the details. Many colleges do not allow underclassmen to have vehicles on campus (for safety, distraction, and space considerations). Other campuses are near large public transportation arteries and therefore want to encourage the use and connection with public transportation. When you are considering your colleges of choice, consider how dependent you are on your vehicle (if you have one) and how much you assume that you will either want to or need to drive during college. Obviously, your cost of attendance at college will increase with ownership and operation of a private vehicle. Also, your capacity to navigate public transportation (or yes, get rides from your new friends who have cars!), will be part of the college learning process dependent upon your choice

Finally, understanding the availability, strength, and academic and employment reputation of your selected colleges in your major fields of study will be key in your college search. About 30-40% of college students are "undeclared" when they first attend college (meaning they have no selected major) and a good number of people change their major while in college. So, the more you can understand about your purpose

and calling (from the earlier chapter), the better equipped you will be to

drill down on major details. Understanding the college you may attend

and how they approach your major field, understanding how they address

transfer credits (if you transfer from one school to another), and how

many major options they have, should be on your list of criterion to

evaluate. Also trying to discern if your selected college has a good

reputation with the employment community around the college and

whether they have specific pathways from the classroom to the workforce

are important. Particularly since the Great Recession of 2006-2010, most

American colleges have tried to strengthen their college-to-career

pathways.

These details can seem mind-numbing. But investigating them

carefully and ensuring that you have asked and answered these questions

to your satisfaction will strengthen your confidence in your final

decision. I hope I'm not belaboring the point too much, but I think

making these decisions on your own is really hard and potentially

dangerous. I strongly urge you to invite others who know you and love you on to this journey and get input from them and have them help you evaluate the options. The choice is yours, but you need to have some great counselors. (Think Proverbs 15:22: "Plans fail for lack of counsel, but with many advisers they succeed.")

Chapter 6

The Argument for a Public College

You have thought long and hard about your dreams, desires, and yes you even considered those confusing details that will make up the analytical part of your journey. You did all that before you stared at the multiple slate mail cards, brochures, emails, and social media interruptions that have come your way since you started your college search. By now, we trust that you have a pretty good sense of clarity about what your values and priorities are. You have some family and friends who will walk this journey with you and they are prepared to help give input and evaluate information and experiences with you.

At this point, I'd like to clarify that I am going to describe the benefits and potential concerns about attending a 4-year college or university. Many states have community (sometimes called "junior") colleges that offer a 2-year pathway to a full 4-year university. Depending on the state you live in, you may have access to these community colleges at a greatly reduced rate. Some community college attenders have had very positive experiences, but others have been challenged with the notion of being able to complete the 2-year program in a timely fashion due to class availability. Finally, there is some research that suggests that 2-year college attenders have a lower graduation rate for 4-year degrees.[7] None of this causes me to be negative on community college attendance, but simply to suggest a clear examination of these matters prior to a decision about where to begin your college experience.

In light of all the data and all the pre-work you have accomplished, why might you consider a public 4-year college? Obviously, each individual college is different, but I can imagine a number of reasons why you might pick a public college. I think the advantages of public higher education are fairly clear, but let me suggest that they organize around 4 likely themes: Cost, Name Recognition, Breadth of Degrees, and Student/Experience Diversity. We'll briefly explore each of these to help position you as you evaluate the potential for public colleges to be on your final selection list.

---

[7]
https://www.forbes.com/sites/prestoncooper2/2017/12/19/college-completion-rates-are-still-disappointing/#79585379263a

The cost of public higher education is greatly variable, dependent upon the state where the school is located and whether you attend as a resident or out of state student. Generally speaking however, a public in-state tuition will be cheaper than a private college tuition, even after financial aid (remember our discussion about "net cost" of tuition/fees after financial aid). While recognizing that each individual school and student is different, I suspect this is generally true. However, it will be important for you to think about whether or not you should include your residential costs if you choose to live on campus. Where I serve (in California), public college attendance AND residential costs can sometimes be roughly equal or only slightly lower than private college costs after financial aid. However, please be sure to check graduation rates as public education is sometimes enrollment impacted and that can slow time to graduation. Generally speaking, all things considered, living at home and attending a public college is the cheapest college attendance option.

Another reason you might want to choose a public college is that of name recognition. Especially if you continue to live in the state of your college choice, it is highly likely that your public college will be well known and will have strong name recognition to future employers and in your social circle. Even though it is very rare, private colleges do occasionally fail due to financial insolvency. It is exceedingly unlikely that a public college will cease to exist (as they are supported by public tax dollars) and therefore you can be confident of your college continuance. As long as your public college of choice has a good reputation, name recognition can very well serve you in the years to come

Most public colleges are quite large and therefore have a variety of degrees to choose from. As we discussed previously, it is not uncommon for a college student to change majors, sometimes more than once! There is an excellent article on the subject worth reading that will give you good background information on the subject on InsideHigherEd.com.[8] The advantage of a large institution is the ability to offer multiple majors, many of which are in fields that may be difficult for private schools to offer. Private schools are much more subject to

---

[8]
https://www.insidehighered.com/news/2017/12/08/nearly-third-students-change-major-within-three-years-math-majors-most

enrollment pressures than public colleges and therefore must offer majors where they can draw a critical mass of students and be able to afford the faculty and support resources for the field of study. Should you choose a public college, one advantage you will have is the relative ease of changing majors to another field of study.

A word to the wise: I often say (as a College President), "If you are going to have a crisis, have it in your sophomore year." What I mean by that is that if you are going to change majors, it is much easier to do it in your freshman or sophomore year and that way you will not lose too much time in attaining your degree (as it is relatively easy to switch majors in the first 2 years where the majority of your coursework is in general education). However, even if it is your junior or senior year, it would be better to change your major towards something you are passionate about and can succeed with than remain with a degree major that you loathe and are uninspired to pursue.

The final rationale for a public college choice is centered around student experience and diversity. Again, given the size of most public colleges as large, it is likely involving a more diverse population. Many public universities have a strong contingent of first-generation college students and a range of socioeconomic statuses represented. Private colleges are continuing to work on these matters, but I think it is fair to say that public colleges are – generally speaking – more ethnically and socioeconomically diverse than the majority of private colleges (again, individual exceptions apply). One final factor in a diverse experience is that the size of public colleges often means an ability to offer a breadth and array of student clubs and activities beyond the scope of most private colleges. Most private colleges are fundamentally narrower in student experience options than are the larger public colleges.

I would be remiss if I did not share a concern about public college education. As you know, my doctorate is from a public college (University of California, Santa Barbara), and I honor the expertise and deserved academic reputation of the great colleges of our time. However, I am deeply concerned with the spiritual climate found on many of the public higher education institutions of our day. As I write in late 2018, the public colleges of the United States are largely antagonistic, hostile, and downright dismissive of people of faith and most particularly are dismissive of Bible-believing people of faith in what might be termed historic orthodox Christianity. Because of the poor foundations of many incoming Christian students, and the abject hostility and patent adversarial relationship of many in the professoriate, I have seen many a Christian shipwreck their faith in the early days of their public college experience.

I have advocated since the early 1980s that any person of Christian faith attending a public college consider strongly the need for 3 things:

1) A well-developed Biblical and Christ-honoring worldview foundation. I suggest a consideration of many excellent programs, including Wheatstone Academy[9] and the resources from the Colson Center.[10]

2) A day-one connection to a strong and thriving local church in the immediate vicinity of the public college of your choice. Many churches in college towns have particularly strong young adult ministries. If you attend a public college, please connect with a

---

[9] https://www.christianadulthood.org
[10] http://www.colsoncenter.org

vibrant church so that you can experience weekly encouragement and Biblical community.

3) Please ensure that the public college of your choosing has a vibrant campus ministry with a trusted and strong organization like InterVarsity, Cru, or Chi Alpha. Being with other students of like faith who are being challenged in classrooms, and being equipped to defend your faith with sincerity and kindness (see 1 Peter 3:15-16), will be essential.

I know many strong followers of Christ who attended public colleges and grew in their faith during this season. If you choose to attend a public college, please do so with consideration of all the factors we discussed AND ensuring your very strong protection and preparation as referenced above.

Chapter 6

The Argument for a Private College

If I am looking for a college to attend, why would I consider a private college? At one level, the assumption might be that the factors are either the same or the opposite of a public college. Actually, a private college (and here we are assuming it is not a faith-based college) has some unique distinctives when compared with public colleges. My experience suggests that the private college that might make it on your list would do so because it has deep subject matter reputation, has a close-knit campus community, and has a small student-faculty ratio.

Almost all private colleges first established in the colonies before the Revolution were established by Christian denominations (except for the University of Pennsylvania). However, many private colleges that were religiously established are now clearly nonsectarian and nonreligious (there are just under 1,900 private colleges in the US with about 1,000 of them retaining some form of religious affiliation, to a greater or lesser degree). Private colleges that have thrived without being faith-based have almost all established some curricular areas where they have some level of renown, at least enough for alumni to support them financially and for them to be considered worthy of contributions by the local business community. As you are exploring private colleges, it is a good question to say "what are you known for academically?" Almost always, there will be 4-5 curricular areas at most, as private colleges are unable to offer the scale of degree programs found in public settings. As long as your degree interests are in alignment with what the private college offers, this can be a positive outcome. Further, if your private college choice has a known area of curricular expertise, future employers may value your degree more highly based on the reputation of the private college you attend.

I used to be a pastor of local churches and I consulted with other local churches. EVERY local church I ever visited said they were "friendly." Interestingly, not everyone who visited those churches experienced that. Private colleges almost always advertise and promote the fact that they have a close-knit student community and that the student experience is their highest value. You will generally find students at private colleges with deeper and richer peer relationships than the general population of a public college (though again, obvious exceptions apply, especially to those engaged in student government or tightly knit social communities on a public campus). The level of campus activities, deepened student relationships, and shared experiences with domestic and international travel, and smaller academic departments all combine to make the campus community a vital part of the private college experience. Private colleges that do well in this dimension make the student experience in the context of their academic and student life activities a central and vital theme of their life.

Professors who teach in a private college tend to make less than their public college counterparts, unless they are in a very elite or larger private college (think Stanford, USC, Princeton, Duke, etc.). It is my experience that faculty at private colleges, even if they have demonstrated research success and experience, prioritize and highly value their teaching roles in a way that is significant. Many students who attend private colleges do so because of the low teacher to student ratio and the belief that they will receive personal attention from their professors. I attended one such school in the late 1970s and it was not uncommon to be in a class with 15-20 people, and fairly frequent to be in a class with 10 or fewer students (by the way, you cannot sleep or be unprepared in those classes!). I know that my life was very personally impacted by the experiences I had as an 18- to 21-year-old student with my PhD professors pouring into my life and academic preparation. The allure of personal and academic conversations with academically gifted and experienced professionals is a profound reason to consider a private college. The contrasting public college experience is to rarely have contact in a large public college with a full professor until your final year; in some settings you will never have contact with any but graduate teaching assistants.

There are many fine private colleges and my life personally, and those of my family, have been shaped by them. Again, I would be remiss if I did not at least call to your attention the reality that the worldview of the people who will be imparting higher education to you is of the utmost importance in my opinion. I am concerned that should you pursue higher education in a private college setting which is by its very nature, more personalized and intimate than a public college setting, it is essential for you to be spiritually prepared and protected on that journey by committing to the 3 disciplines I referenced in the previous chapter (worldview training, thriving local church, vital campus ministry).

Yes, I am biased. But, I told you that at the beginning. So, if you are still with me, you probably are at least willing to hear my case for a faith-based college education. As you do, I hope you'll hear me out as my framework has been developed over 40+ years on the journey.

Chapter 7

The Argument for a Faith-Based College

Since you already know my bias, you probably expect me to really go "after it" in this chapter. And, I hope you will not be disappointed. I plan to! However, before I begin sharing why I think you should consider a faith-based college, I want to replay a vivid recollection from my own memory banks.

I was 17 years old, sitting in a freshman class, *Introduction to the Old Testament.* It was my first year in college and I was a young student (I had skipped a grade in elementary school). I went to a college that had been founded by a faith group and they communicated that they were a Christian school. Within about the first 20 minutes of the class, the professor (who had a PhD from a respected private college) said these words, "There might have been an Abraham." Because I was precocious, a Baptists pastor's son, and yes, had my Bible with me, I remember shooting my hand up in the air and saying, "umm, excuse me. It says right here in Genesis 12, God told Abram to go ye therefore to a land that I will show you." Her response was, "So, why do you believe that?" At that moment, I thought I was engaged in some form of college level debate so I began to answer her question with the precious little that I knew about Biblical historicity. After a couple minutes of my admittedly weak response, she proceeded to tell me and the whole class that Abraham had never existed as a historical person, that Moses had not written the first 5 books of the Old Testament, and that writing did not even exist at the time of Moses. I was to later read all of these same assertions from the book authored by an Ivy League professor that was to serve as our textbook.

The professor's assertions did not shake my faith (they made me mad!), but they did shake my understanding of whether I was in a Christian school. So, I committed to studying apologetics throughout my college career and become a capable apologist for the historicity and reasonableness of the Christian faith. As an aside, the assertions of the professor in my late 1970s class were categorically untrue, at least demonstrably in the notion of writing not existing at the time of Moses (circa 1400 BC). The code of Hammurabi is a complex legal code, and it was written at approximately 1800 BC (about 400 years prior to Moses).

The code of Hammurabi was discovered in 1901, about 70 years before my college textbook was published. So, what is my point? If you are going to choose a faith-based school, make sure you know the Biblical worldview and the faith framework before you attended. I did not and ended up with a challenging college experience. While my experience did not shake my faith, I had very strong resources (family, friends, and church) that equipped me to complete my education and go on for my ultimate calling (and in a good news note, it was what motivated me to get a doctorate from a public university).

So, I want you to consider attending a faith-based college where you can grow spiritually and discover all that God made you to be. I want you to be able to pursue your dreams and experience dynamic spiritual life. I think a great faith-based school can do that for you and in you. For the rest of this chapter, I'm going to tell you the 3 things that our faith-based school Jessup University tries to provide. We do lots of things well, but I think we do these 3 particularly well:

1). We equip you to Thrive Spiritually: When I speak about it publicly, I will often say that we believe that college is a time when your faith should be built up not torn down. I think that when you attend a Christian faith-based college, your education should be unequivocally Christ-Centered and about His Word, and His work in the world. One definition of "learning" is "change." I think that spiritual change (or transformation) should be a dynamic part of the spiritual growth journey in college. Your student life experience at a faith-based college should support your discovery and growth in your walk with God. Here are a few markers I look for:

- Are the people who lead your potential faith-based school passionately in love with Jesus?

- Is the school deeply committed to Biblical Authority? Jesus is the Word incarnate, Scripture is the Word given by inspiration of God for us (see 2 Timothy 3:16). All Christians recognize that Jesus-loving and Bible believing Christians disagree on some matters of interpretation, but the core of the faith is unquestioned. Does your potential school believe in absolute truth and proclaim it boldly? Do they represent historic orthodoxy in their worldview, teaching, and policy behaviors?

- Is your school committed to a John 17 relationship of unity with the local church? We all recognize the local church, made up of people like us, is fundamentally flawed. Does your potential school live in humility and grace with one another and are the people committed to a local body of believers where they can love, grow, serve, and manifest the life of Christ in their local communities?

2). Will your potential faith-based school give you a strong foundation in the liberal arts? I am a firm believer in the liberal arts. Long ago, I came to understand that all truth is God's Truth, that all beauty is a (poor) reflection of the ultimate beauty of the Creator, and all art is a (poor) symbol of the ultimate Artist. I was fortunate to learn at an early age that God is infinite and we are finite. Our conceptions of God are always necessarily limited by our finite understandings. At the same time, I learned early that we did not suffer alone in a world where the Creator would choose to remain mysterious and unknowable. Instead, we live in a world in which the Creator has revealed Himself.

Our Creator has revealed Himself in the created world, in the written Word of God, and in Jesus – the Living Word of God. This general, special, and incarnate revelation of God means that He wants to be known and that He has made Truth available to us. In fact, Jesus tells us to love Him with all our "heart, soul, mind, and strength" (Matthew 22:37). This understanding of God as the one who reveals Himself, and as the source of all Truth, is at the heart of the liberal arts. There is no branch of knowledge that does not have its source in Him, nor is there any discipline of study about which God does not loudly proclaim "MINE!" (a riff on a line from a Dutch reformed theologian, Abraham Kuyper).

At the school I lead, we have articulated our specific University Learning Goals to explicitly address these matters; I share them here not to get you to come to our school (though we'd love that!), but to encourage you to ask for these from any school you consider:

Jessup University Learning Goals:

Articulate the relevance of Jesus Christ, His teachings, and a Biblical

worldview to their personal and professional lives.

Communicate effectively across cultures.

Demonstrate critical, analytical, and creative thinking.

Exhibit competence in their chosen disciplines.

Engage in a lifelong pursuit of knowledge, character formation, and

service to their local and global communities.

Before I share the 3rd thing on which I think your potential

faith-based school should be evaluated, let me share what I think is the

future direction of higher education in America. In 2011, I began my

journey as a President of a faith-based college. Of all the books I have

read, the one that has spoken most concretely on the subject of

innovation is *The Innovative University* by Christensen and Eyring.

From that book, and from my other readings, interactions, and personal reflection, I have come to believe that the future of higher education is FDA.

Flexible ~ Distributed ~ Affordable

Every once in a while, I will think of myself as a "serial reductionist." It is part of what I do. I try to take complex matters and make them simple. And lest you think I am unaware, let me point out that I know that some things are irreducibly complex. Yes, I know that making things seem simple sometimes does a disservice to the inquirer and to the subject. But, if you'll humor me, I think we can all be helped by thinking about the future of higher education and Jessup in FDA terms. Let me explain what I mean by each of these terms.

Flexible. Do you remember the phrase "banker's hours"? If you are old enough to remember the phrase, you know that is an antiquated phrase. Today's bankers work long hours and their online services are 24/7. The future of higher education will become increasingly flexible relative to the WHEN, the WHO, the WHERE, and the HOW. Space does not allow me to describe all the ways this is true, but suffice it to say that there are many colleges where courses are being offered at all hours of the day and night, reaching a dizzying variety of student types, "classrooms" of assorted types, and through every modality including face to face, online, hybrid, and in what is now called "massive online courses" with tens of thousands of students. This flexibility will not only continue, it will accelerate. The future of higher education is flexible.

Distributed. Following closely on the heels of the notion of *Flexible,* is the idea of *Distributed.* I view this as a required fundamental shift in the mind of the university. Education is not WHERE I (as the university) say it is, it is WHERE the student is. In other words, I believe the future of higher education will be distributed in ways and places that the learner chooses. Yes, I want to be face to face in a classroom on a campus. And, I want to be online at 2 a.m. And, I want to be at my favorite coffee shop or workplace with my learning cohort. All for the same class. Whereas previously, learners had to seek out teachers where they were, now teachers are going to be meeting students where they are and want to be and mediated through technology and social connections that are of the learners choosing and not the teacher's alone. The future of higher education is distributed.

Affordable. The cost of tuition increasing far beyond inflation rates, the lack of reasonable graduation rates by many schools, and the student loan debt of college graduates relative to their workplace earnings have combined to create a national conversation about the value of a college degree. Without giving you my opinions on all of these things (yes, I have some!), let me suggest simply that a college degree has to be "affordable." What do I mean by that? I mean it in fundamental economic and social terms. A college degree has value. Virtually everyone agrees with that. The question is, how much value does a college degree have? The intangible value has to do with character, integration of faith and knowledge, developmental maturity, critical thinking skills, etc. The tangible value has to do with what job skills and employment results from a college degree. In other words, "affordable" relates both to the economic capacity of the buyer and the value the marketplace puts on the particular degree and institution that awards it.

I think we are heading to a future in higher education where learning AND employment outcomes will be factored in to the price of a university education. "Affordable" means that we will see variable pricing on degrees and schools based on learning outcomes and employment earnings outcomes as well. The market will more quickly punish, in the future, those schools that do not have the right equilibrium between the intangible and tangible benefits of their university education. The future of higher education is affordable.

And now, the 3rd question for your potential faith-based college:
3). Will your school make you exceptionally employable? I am well aware of the conversation and debate regarding the difference between education and training. Many who have heard me speak about exceptionally employable have gently suggested that maybe 'exceptionally employable" is not a good aspiration for a liberal arts university. You know the old stories about liberal arts graduates having to find work in the fast food or retail industries because they are not employable elsewhere. You know the other side of the argument, where

the university is always resistant to change and prepares students for the world that passed 2 decades ago when its professors were graduating from college. I have opinions about both thoughts. I think they are both wrong.

Those who know my background know that I have almost 40 years in some form of pastoral ministry. People regularly ask me the question, "In the Great Commission, which is more important – evangelism or discipleship?" My answer is always YES! BOTH are absolutely vital. You can't have discipleship without evangelism, and evangelism without discipleship violates the John 16 exhortation to bear fruit that remains. I think the same way about university education. University education equips students with the ability to think, read, write, and speak well, among other disciplines. I am also deeply devoted to the notion that faith-based colleges produce servant leaders engaged in the work of transformation. That transformative work happens in us personally, in organizations we lead and serve, and in our culture.

So, I do NOT see any conflict between having a quality liberal arts education and being exceptionally employable; in fact, quite the opposite. Many employers will trust graduates from faith-based schools based on demonstrated character and work ethic. In the fall of 2011, I attended a WSCUC (our accreditation agency) briefing where research was shared from 2010 regarding what employers are looking for:

Critical thinking and analytic reasoning	81%
Complex problem solving	75%
Teamwork skills in diverse groups	71%
Creativity and innovation	70%
Information literacy	68%
Quantitative reasoning	63%

I'm convinced that those skills are well taught in faith-based liberal arts universities that are thriving spiritually with a quality liberal arts education, equipping you to be exceptionally employable. At the very minimum, if you are a follower of Christ, my sincere hope is that you will consider a faith-based school in your college search. But, I most of all want you to be in a college that is the exact *Right Choice* for you...so let's talk a bit about you for a moment in the next chapter.

Chapter 9

Challenging You To Be You

(Previously published in my book *Finding Your Place in God's Plan*[11])

Unless you are careful, somebody will press you into a mold that doesn't fit you. Unless you're careful, somebody will have you run a race that is not yours to run. Unless you're careful, you will take on an assignment that is not yours. The fact is that God did not make you average. You are a perfect fit for the place God has designed especially for you, and He's given you gifts to joyfully fulfill that place.

Let me tell you a story about an animal school.

Once upon a time, the animals decided they must do something heroic to meet the problems of "a new world." So they organized a school.

They had adopted an activity curriculum consisting of running, climbing, swimming, and flying. To make it easier to administer the curriculum, all the animals took all the subjects.

---

[11] Jackson, John, *Finding Your Place in God's Plan*, Nashville, Abingdon Press, 2009

The duck was excellent in swimming. In fact better than his instructor,

but he made only passing grades in flying and was very poor in running.

Since he was slow in running, he had to stay after school and also drop

swimming in order to practice running. This kept up until his webbed feet

were badly worn and he was only average in swimming. But average was

acceptable in school so nobody worried about that, except the duck.

The rabbit started at the top of the class in running but had a

nervous breakdown because of so much makeup work in swimming.

The squirrel was excellent in climbing until he developed

frustration in the flying class where his teacher made him start from the

ground up instead of from the treetop down. He also developed a charley

horse from overexertion and then got a C in climbing and D in running.

The eagle was a problem child and was disciplined severely. In the

climbing class, he beat all the others to the top of the tree but insisted on

using his own way to get there.

At the end of the year, an abnormal eel that could swim

exceedingly well, and also run, climb, and fly a little had the highest

average and was valedictorian.

The prairie dogs stayed out of school and fought the tax levy because the administration would not add digging and burrowing to the curriculum. They apprenticed their children to a badger and later joined the groundhogs and gophers to start a successful private school.[12]

Only God judges perfectly. We look at the world through imperfect eyes, through our own flawed perspectives. We make judgments about other people based on our faulty views. We think we have enough information about others to make right judgments, but we don't. We make this mistake in the world and in the church as well. In 1 Corinthians 4:1–5, the apostle Paul addressed this issue of judging the service of others. The duty of a servant is to manage the master's affairs so that the purposes of the master are realized. A servant must be faithful to the master's trust. The Corinthian believers were being critical of Paul's ministry. He told them that their evaluation of him was irrelevant and that even his own evaluation of his performance may be faulty. What

---

[12] Reavis, George H., *The Animal School*,

www.surfaquarium.com/presentations/MI.pdf

mattered was God's evaluation of his service. Only God has enough information to make accurate judgments. Paul wrote:

This, then, is how you ought to regard us: as servants of Christ and as those entrusted with the mysteries God has revealed. Now it is required that those who have been given a trust must prove faithful. I care very little if I am judged by you or by any human court; indeed, I do not even judge myself. My conscience is clear, but that does not make me innocent. It is the Lord who judges me. Therefore, judge nothing before the appointed time; wait until the Lord comes. He will bring to light what is hidden in darkness and will expose the motives of the heart. At that time each will receive their praise from God.

Paul said there will come a time when we stand before God. It will not be important then what other people think of us – as important as it may seem right now. It will not even be important then what we think of ourselves. What will be important at the end of all time is what God thinks of us. The truth is that we are all common vessels. None of us is fine china. Nevertheless, each of us has been entrusted with God's heavenly treasure. In 2 Corinthians 4:7, Paul remarked how amazing it is that God puts heavenly treasure in ordinary vessels (cracked pots, like you and me). We all have issues – yet God places heavenly treasure in us anyway. God will examine our motives, not our appearance. God sees inside our hearts. He understands our intentions. Whereas we make judgments on the externals of people, God does not. Is the intent of your heart to serve Him and to be faithful to Him?

In 1 Corinthians 3:10–11, Paul wrote, *"By the grace God has given me, I laid a foundation as a wise builder, and someone else is building on it. But each one should build with care. For no one can lay any foundation other than the one already laid, which is Jesus Christ."* In this passage, Paul was talking about establishing the local church in Corinth, where he had laid the foundation on the gospel of Jesus Christ – the only true foundation. Other leaders after Paul continued the spiritual "construction" of the church at Corinth. Paul was warning people to be careful how they built into the local church.

By application, we can take Paul's warning and examine how we are building our own spiritual lives. Like construction workers, we are building our lives on some foundation. Only one foundation lasts for all eternity, that is, the foundation of a relationship with God through Jesus Christ. Sometimes people refer to this lasting foundation as a "crutch." But, everyone has a crutch, whether it's self-reliance, financial success, social position, prestige, or power. So the question is this: On which foundation are you building your life – an eternal foundation or a temporary one?

Paul's warning continued: *If anyone builds on this foundation using gold, silver, costly stones, wood, hay or straw, his work will be shown for what it is, because the Day will bring it to light. It will be revealed with fire, and the fire will test the quality of each person's work. If what has been built survives, the builder will receive a reward. If it is burned up, the builder will suffer loss but yet will be saved—even though only as one escaping through the flames.* (1 Corinthians 3:12–15)

This passage teaches that it is possible to build on the foundation of Christ using either material, superior or inferior. We can serve God in superior ways or in inferior ways. We can spend our time achieving eternal goals or temporal goals. Paul encouraged believers to build the church using durable materials that would stand the test of the holy fire of the Lord's judgment. In that judgment day, our worthless deeds will be consumed, and we will suffer loss of reward; our eternal deeds will endure the fire, and we will be rewarded accordingly. God will finally expose the work of His servants. No servant will suffer the loss of salvation ("the builder will suffer loss but yet will be saved"), only the loss of reward. So, God wants us to build on the foundation of Christ using superior materials (godly deeds). God wants us to faithfully use in the church the gifts He has given us, for the good of others and for His glory. Then, one day God will judge our construction project – and He will judge perfectly.

Several years ago, I helped an older and wiser friend do some repair work on a roof. I told my friend, "You know, I'm not very good at this." He replied, "That's OK, I just need an extra pair of hands. All you have to do is carry things and do what I tell you to do. It will be a piece of cake." My friend then picked up a chalk line and said, "Take this end of the chalk line to the other end of the roof; then I'll snap it to make a perfectly straight line." I went to the other side, but at first, I didn't hold the line tightly enough. My friend started to get frustrated because he knew that every step of the process was important. An inferior line would result in an inferior roof. When I finally got my end of the line taut, he snapped a straight line, and we began the roofing project.

I never went into the roofing business, but I learned a critical lesson that day. God holds the chalk line of my life in a secure, solid way. He has a project in mind that He has perfectly designed for me. I'm on the other end of the chalk line, but I just might be dawdling around, preventing Him from snapping a perfectly straight line for the project. I must hold the line tightly and follow His straight line to complete the project to His approval.

Know this: God loves you and watches over you daily. He is doing a miracle of transformation in your soul. So, grab your end of the chalk line, pull tightly, and follow the straight and narrow line that He snaps, because the miracles that will follow and the fruit you will bear will delight your heavenly Father, the church He established, and you,

His beloved child. Whatever your role is in the church and the Kingdom of God – whether you are an elbow or an arm or a wrist or a hand or fingers or an ear or a foot – you are perfectly suited to the treasure He has entrusted to you. One day you will stand before your loving heavenly Father and all your service will be brought to light. Your faithful work will become evident, and you will receive praise for your loyal service.

Chapter 10

Make Your Decision and Lean In!

By this point in the journey, it is my hope that you have reviewed the piles of materials, have visited the websites, and you have a list of schools that you have narrowed down to choose between. It might be 5-10 schools, or it might be 2-3. I strongly suggest you not look at more than 10 schools as you will likely not make a better choice, but you will most certainly get more confused.

So what do you do in the final analysis process? I'd like to suggest a quick "order of operations" that will bring this decision process home for you:

1) **Pray.**

2) **Clarify your Dreams/Desires/Details Metrics**…and remember that this is about your hopes and dreams and the uniqueness of you and your life. Develop your lists with input from those around you who know you, but do not chase the dreams or desires of others you have read about or seen in publications.

3) **Visit** at least your top 3 schools (my personal sense is that visiting more than 5 schools just gets confusing).

4) **Give** yourself some time.

5) **Apply** to your top 3-5 schools.

6) **Receive Acceptances and Aid Offers** for your chosen schools.

7) **Pray and Receive Counsel.**

8) **Make Your Decision.**

Celebrate!

Lean in and Rejoice in Your Choice

Big decisions like faith (who will you trust today and for all eternity?), college, marriage (who will you choose as your partner on this life's journey?), vocation, and many others are complex and multi-faceted. But you can do this! The journey will absolutely NOT be a straight line. I promise you in advance, and even as you have thought about the various aspects in our short journey covered in this book, that things will happen that you did not anticipate and could not have predicted. Life is a journey and navigating the unknowns and unexpected turns is part of what makes one fully human and fully mature. There is no human formula for living a "mistake free" life, but I believe that we have outlined several key aspects of decision making that I hope you will take to heart. Let me review them here:

1) Pray. I think the first step in making great decisions is to give up. Give up the notion that you are the ruler of the universe or even your world. Submit and surrender your life to God in the person and work of Jesus Christ. Check out whoisjesus-really.com for a basic overview.

2) Discern. Part of making great decisions is to understand who you are and what it is that you value. The Bible says to "guard your heart, for it is the wellspring of life." (Proverbs 4:23) Knowing who you are and what you value will help you establish your "north star" of your personal values and priorities.

3) Examine. Great decisions typically involve lots of data and details. Embrace this part of decision making. Understand the importance of getting a variety of inputs and ensuring that you are surrounded by people who know you and love you. Great decisions are rarely (if ever!) made alone.

4) Decide. Yes, you will eventually have to "pull the trigger" and make your decision. I hope you pray and ponder (you'll do that a lot!). But eventually you have to decide. When you decide, know in advance that you will feel a sense of relief that a decision has been made but also know that you may have a bit of uncertainty that you wonder if the options that you eliminated were the better choices. "Never looking back" sounds good on paper, but most of us who make major decisions do so with humility knowing that we are imperfect people and we might make a mistake in any given decision. Mistakes are rarely fatal and if you make one, you will get through it!

5) Celebrate and implement. I strongly suggest that you give yourself some time to rejoice! Gather friends and family and "mark the moment" of major life decisions. Then, the real work begins. Implement your decision and all the myriad details that go along with it. Implementation will not be a straight line either, but remember all the reasons why you chose the way you did.

Enjoy! My prayer is that your choice of a college will be a thrilling and life changing decision in every best sense of those words. I pray that you will sense the presence of God and great joy in deciding this choice with those who know you and love and care for you. Your life is a great journey, not unlike a sailboat on the sea. You will face contrary headwinds and glorious bursts of supportive tailwinds. In each and every season, you can rejoice in knowing that you are not alone, you are loved, and you have a fantastic future in front of you. Decide well and decide for life!

If you would like additional resources from Dr. John Jackson, please visit our site at www.drjohnjackson.com

Dr. Jackson is also the other of several additional titles on leadership and transformation that you can find on Amazon:

High Impact Church Planting

Pastorpreneur

God-Size Your Church

Leveraging Your Leadership Style

Leveraging Your Communication Style

Finding Your Place in God's Plan

If you would like to book Dr. Jackson for speaking arrangements or consulting with your organization, please contact him at

info@drjohnjackson.com

Made in the
USA
Lexington, KY